The
Premier Collection

1950s and 1960s SOUTHERN STEAM IN COLOUR

Terry Cole

www.crecy.co.uk

© Terry Cole 2015

ISBN 9781906419875

First published in 2015 by Crécy Publishing Ltd

A CIP record for this book is available from the British Library

Publisher's note: Every effort has been made to identify and correctly attribute photographic credits. Any error that may have occurred is entirely unintentional.

Printed in Malta by Gutenberg Press Ltd

**Noodle Books is an imprint of
Crécy Publishing Limited**
1a Ringway Trading Estate
Shadowmoss Road
Manchester M22 5LH

www.crecy.co.uk

Front cover 'U' Class 2-6-0 No 31613 arrives at Horsebridge with a train from Cheltenham via the Midland & South Western Junction route and destined for Southampton Terminus. (The coaches are the giveaway, being former GWR designs repainted in then standard BR maroon.) Horsebridge was a station that served very little; there was no village nearby, but it was the nearest the railway got to the larger settlement of Kings Somborne. The line from Andover to Romsey via Horsebridge closed in September 1964, although trains from the MSWJ had already ceased to run after September 1961. *Noodle Books collection*

Rear cover main image 'A1X' No 32670 pauses between shunting operations at Rolvenden in 1953. The engine still carries a faded green livery and the former private-owner wagon clearly shows evidence of its previous owner. *Terry Cole collection*

Rear cover small images from top
'Terrier time', the Hayling line in 1961. *Mark Warburton courtesy Mrs Margaret Warburton*

The last main line. When rebuilt the intention was for the Bulleid type to remain in service until the 1970s but electrification would soon sweep away this Southampton scene.
Mark Warburton courtesy Mrs M Warburton

A rarity from the 1950s, E5X No 32570.
Terry Cole Collection

And a survivor, one of the Adams radial tanks at home on the Lyme Regis branch. *Mark Warburton courtesy Mrs Margaret Warburton*

Publisher's/Author's note
Every effort has been made to correctly attribute ownership/copyright of the images used within this work. If an error has occurred this is entirely unintentional. A number of images were also obtained from the collections of deceased individuals, which makes correct sourcing even more difficult.

Contents

Introduction

I t is well over half a century now since the heyday of British Railways steam, that period in the 1950s and '60s when steam still reigned supreme and neither the Modernisation Plan nor the blue-grey corporate image had taken full effect. Looking back now, it was a period of incredible diversity. The Southern had been investing heavily in electrification and as a result a large section of its locomotive fleet remained unmodernised. Despite substantial withdrawals after the war, the company still had an enormous number of different classes, mostly from the three pre-Grouping companies. In this volume I want to explore and remember that golden age.

So what to include in a 'Premier Collection'? Over the years there has been much good material published, but I wanted to include a sizeable proportion of new, fresh material that had not been seen before. I also wanted not just to present the final few years of steam but to include as much material as possible from the 1950s. Finding new material from this period is not easy. Colour film was extremely expensive, cameras more so, and therefore beyond the reach of most enthusiasts. So I am grateful to those photographers, in many cases unknown, who recorded the scene. Fortunately the early film stock has proved to be extremely robust and has usually reached us in excellent condition.

I wanted this collection to record not just the locomotives but also the railway within the landscape – scenes featuring working trains, ordinary trains for the most part, going about their business. I wanted to reawaken those memories, half-forgotten, of a train glimpsed from a bridge, from a platform or from a road.

How far I have succeeded in these aims is for you, the reader, to judge. My hope is that this is a book you will want to go back to again and again. On winter evenings, when there is nothing on television, I hope you will settle down in your favourite chair with your favourite drink and this book to treat yourself to an evening of pure nostalgia. If you do I have succeeded, and this will indeed be a 'Premier Collection'.

Terry Cole
Steyning, August 2015

N15 'King Arthur' Class No 30806 *Sir Galleron* powers through Sittingbourne in the 1950s with a Margate express formed of BR Mark 1 coaches and two Pullman cars. *Alan Sainty collection*

Class 'U1' No 31897 heads a Margate express near Shortlands Junction in July 1956, formed of a mixture of BR Mark 1 and Bulleid coaches in BR crimson and cream livery. The 21 members of the class, which was a three-cylinder development of the 'U' Class, were introduced in 1928 precisely for this sort of work. *Terry Cole collection*

The Westerham branch

The SER branch to Westerham left the main line to Hastings at Dunton Green and had two intermediate halts at Chevening and Brasted. In many respects it was a typical South Eastern branch line. After the 'R' and 'R1' tanks were withdrawn, 'H' Class 0-4-4 tanks monopolised the services. However, a wide variety of coaching stock could be seen until closure in 1961. There was a brief attempt to run the branch as a 'preserved line', but the powers that be had their eyes on the trackbed for use as part of the M25 so the scheme failed.

Here we see 'H' Class No 31517 at Dunton Green on 10 September 1960 waiting in the Westerham branch platform with a push-pull train composed of ex-LSWR 'Emigrant' coaches still in the early BR red livery. These coaches, which were originally built in the early 1900s to carry emigrants on their way from Eastern Europe to the New World, were converted into push-pull trains in the 1930s. Their short length and possession of a corridor throughout made them ideal for branch-line use, as the guard could collect the fares from passengers boarding at wayside stations during the journey. *Terry Cole collection*

'H' Class No 31519 waits at Brasted station on its way to Westerham on 20 March 1960. The two-coach train is an ex-LBSCR push-pull set, again still in early BR red livery. It is clear from this photograph that the facilities provided here where much more substantial than for your average halt. The brown lorry parked in front of the station adds a further vintage touch. *Terry Cole collection*

No 31518, another 'H' Class locomotive, is just arriving at Chevening Halt with the 1.03pm service from Westerham on 4 June 1960. The train is also formed of an ex-LBSCR push-pull set. Ex-SECR 'Railmotor' sets were also often used on the line. *Terry Cole collection*

'H' Class 31517 enters Westerham station on 10 September 1960. The station consisted of a single platform, a run-round loop and a goods yard, which can be seen to the right. In the yard there was also an original SER goods signal, which survived to the end. This train is probably the same as the one photographed at Dunton Green, as the crew haven't put a headcode disc on the front. After all, everyone knew where the train was going! *Terry Cole collection*

Ashford shed

Ashford was the hub of the South Eastern system, so it is perhaps not surprising to find a number of colour pictures taken there. In this view, taken on 2 October 1955, 'L' Class No 31772, an Ashford resident, has been cleaned and is being prepared for duty. Next to it can be seen a tender (probably of an 'N' Class 'Mogul') still carrying the first British Railways livery with Southern Railway Bulleid-style lettering. *Terry Cole collection*

Also being prepared at its home shed on the same day is 'L1' Class 4-4-0 No 31759. *Terry Cole collection*

Ashford maintained a South Eastern feel to the end. In this general view taken in the early 1960s, 'H' Class No 31263 and 'C' Class No 31510 stand out of steam while 'C' Class No 31690 is in the line of engines being prepared. *Kevin Robertson collection*

Tonbridge and Tunbridge Wells

Brighton-built Standard Class 4 tank No 80151 leaves Tonbridge Tunnel with a train made up of narrow Maunsell stock. Burning coal may not be environmentally friendly, but there is no doubting the value of the wildlife corridors that the railways provided – the ox-eye daisies are a very prominent feature in this early-summer photo. *Terry Cole collection*

'U1' Class No 31892 stands at the imposing Tunbridge Wells West station with a Brighton to Tonbridge train made up of a Maunsell four-coach 'Restriction 1' set. To the east end of the station was Grove Tunnel, which was narrow so stock wider than 'Restriction 1' was barred from going through it. No 31892 was withdrawn towards the end of 1962. *Terry Cole collection*

The Folkestone Harbour branch

The line from Folkestone Harbour to Folkestone Junction was only short but involved a vicious gradient and a severe axle-load restriction that prevented main-line engines from using it. As a result its operation became the preserve of the former South Eastern Railway 'R1' 0-6-0 tanks. To haul a heavy boat train up from the Harbour to the Junction required up to four of these locomotives: two or three at the front with another banking at the rear. By the mid-1950s there were five distinct variants within the ten members of the class. In this 1956 view, two engines with a low dome and Wainwright cab, possibly Nos 31328 and 31340, battle up the incline with a boat train. *Terry Cole collection*

'R1' No 31107, with tall chimney and dome and Wainwright cab, banks an up boat train. The rearmost coach is an ex-SECR 'Continental' brake painted in the early version of BR red and cream livery with the wide red stripe at the top of the side. *Alan Sainty collection*

'R1' No 31337 waits at Folkestone Harbour station with what appears to be an enthusiasts' special. A bowler-hatted inspector is giving the driver some instructions. No 31337 was withdrawn in February 1960. *Terry Cole collection*

Two 'R1s', Nos 31337 and 31047, are busily engaged in shunting at Folkestone Junction in 1954. A variety of coach types can be seen – how many can you identify?
Alan Sainty collection

London termini

Waiting for the signal to back out of Charing Cross station is 'Schools' Class No 30905 *Tonbridge* in early BR black livery, having brought in a train from Hastings.
Terry Cole collection

'Lord Nelson' Class No 30858 *Lord Duncan* stands in Waterloo station carrying a Plymouth headcode. The locomotive has the early BR 'lion and wheel' emblem, so this is probably the mid-1950s. Passengers laden with suitcases await another train on a nearby platform. *Terry Cole collection*

'U' Class No 31639 has just arrived at Victoria Central Section with what appears to be empty stock. The train is formed of a special excursion set (probably 212) with Maunsell 'Nondescript' brake coaches at the ends. There appear to be reservation labels in the windows. In the adjacent platform can be seen part of a DMU forming a train to Uckfield or East Grinstead. Who remembers the News Theatre? I do! *Kevin Robertson collection*

All dressed up and ...

...raring to go! British Railways Standard 'Britannia' Class No 70004 *William Shakespeare* stands expectantly at London Victoria's Platform 8 with the down 'Golden Arrow'. Two new 'Britannias' were allocated to Stewarts Lane shed in the first half of the 1950s to work this prestige service. The driver is sparing a minute to have a chat with a wheel-tapper who has doubtless just checked his train. Wheel-tappers were once a familiar sight at main-line stations before ultrasonic testing. They would walk down a waiting train tapping each wheel in turn; a ringing note meant the wheel was OK, anything else and the wheel was flawed. *Terry Cole collection*

...waiting to go! Stewarts Lane always had a reputation for turning out immaculate locomotives, especially for special events. Here 'Schools' No 30926 *Repton* has had the 'full treatment'. Just look at that copper, brass and steel, and the front coupling and those buffers! Wow, that wasn't achieved in five minutes with a quick rub. The paintwork positively sizzles, too. Driver Miles poses proudly in front of his steed in his best set of overalls; his fireman is also smartly turned out and is wearing a tie. The photograph was taken on 31 May 1961 and the loco is destined to haul a Royal special. Actually, a spare set of buffers and couplings were kept in this condition and swapped onto any engine on 'Royal' duty, and woe betide any crew who marked them. *Terry Cole collection*

...nowhere to go! Meanwhile down in Chipstead sidings on the same day ex-LBSCR 'K' Class No 32340 is on Royal Train standby duty awaiting the call to glory, which never came. She too is 'all bulled up' probably by her home shed of Brighton, which was not going to be outdone by 'The Lane' should its loco be needed. The brightwork may not be as good, but the paintwork is in immaculate ex-works finish – pretty impressive for a 'goods' engine. Who said all locomotives were dirty in the 1960s? Both *Repton* and No 32340 were withdrawn in December of the following year. *Terry Cole collection*25

Central Section shed scenes

'E3' 0-6-2T No 32166 is on the disposal road at Norwood Junction shed with mountains of clinker alongside the pit, witness to many fire cleanings. The clinker shovel rests up against the side of the cab while the fireman is probably using the dart to break up the rest of the clinker. Wielding one of these long shovels in the confines of the cab was not easy, especially when it got red hot! The outside 'skin' on the tanks, a characteristic of all 'Brighton' locos, has been removed, probably due to rusting, to reveal the riveted side tanks beneath. Beyond a 'C2X' moves on for water and coal. No 32166 was withdrawn in September 1959. *Alan Sainty collection*

This is Three Bridges shed on 5 May 1961. On the left is 'Q' Class No 30544, only recently allocated to the depot, and in the centre is long-time resident 'K' Class No 32353. Behind are some 'C2Xs', several out of traffic. On the right is Standard Class 4 No 76005. The shed had a number of freight duties to cover in central Sussex and the surrounding area as well as passenger turns to East Grinstead and beyond. *Terry Cole collection*

Here is No 32353 again on the Bognor Regis turntable. After electrification this depot did not even merit the status of sub-shed. Its servicing facilities were, however, retained for use by locomotives of freight workings and also by the engines of steam passenger excursions to Littlehampton and Bognor during the summer months. At the end of a short branch line from Barnham, the depot was discretely out of the way. It was here that the ill-fated 'Leader' locomotives were stored for a time prior to being towed away for breaking up. *Noodle Books collection*

Brighton station shed and works were all built in an extremely confined space on the side of a steep hill. On the west side of the site were towering chalk cliffs, whereas across on the east site the whole works area had to be built up on piles. The site also restricted movements from one side of the station to the other, the only means of doing so being via the short Platform 3 or equally short adjacent siding. This is an operating restriction that continues to this day. Not that this is obvious in this view taken from Platform 2. The shed is to our left and the station can be seen on the right as 'E4' No 32475 eases forward into the shed yard headshunt on 31 May 1961. A 6-PUL unit on a non-stop working to London can just be glimpsed in the background. *Terry Cole collection*

In this 1950s view 'E5X' No 32570 has been lit up and stands in the shed yard awaiting its turn of duty. That might be station pilot or a pick-up freight working along the east or west coast lines. There was plenty of work at this period to keep Brighton's collection of 0-6-2 tanks busy. No 32570 was withdrawn in January 1956. *Terry Cole collection*

East Grinstead (High Level)

British Railways Standard Class 4 tank No 80085 stands at East Grinstead High Level station on a sunny morning in September 1964 carrying the Oxted line headcode. Lines used to radiate from here to all four points of the compass. After the closure of the lines to Three Bridges and on to Tunbridge Wells, the High Level station was demolished, leaving just the Low Level for trains to Oxted and London. Now the Bluebell Railway extension to East Grinstead is open it is once more possible to travel southwards. *Terry Cole*

An earlier photo at East Grinstead High Level, looking in the opposite direction, shows Fairburn 2-6-4 tank No 42082. This nominally LMS engine was built at Brighton in January 1951 and stayed on the Southern based at Bricklayers Arms until the end of the 1950s. *Terry Cole collection*

Redhill

'D' Class No 31574 has just arrived with a train from Tonbridge in May 1956; the fireman is busy pulling some coal forward, and the driver is having a rest. No 31574 was withdrawn in October of that year. *Terry Cole collection*

'L' Class No 31780 and an unidentified 'D' Class head through Redhill station on their way to the shed in 1955. Although in the heart of 'Brighton' territory, Redhill was a South Eastern station and shed. The tentacles of the SECR extended from Tonbridge through Redhill and Guildford to join the Great Western at Reading. *Terry Cole collection*

The Steyning line

The Steyning line connected the Arun valley line at Horsham with the west coastal line at Shoreham. Here ex-LMS Class 2 2-6-2 tank No 41325 is entering Partridge Green station with a train from Brighton to Horsham. The goods yard is to the left and the South Downs can be seen in the far distance. Today the site is an industrial estate. *Terry Cole collection*

Another '41xxx' tank is seen here entering West Grinstead in the spring of 1964 with a train for Brighton. The delightful signal box is pure unmodified 'Brighton'. Goods facilities have already been withdrawn and the goods yard disconnected. Today the trackbed forms part of the 'Downslink' footpath. *Terry Cole*

The Midhurst branch

Bulleid-designed 'Q1' Class 0-6-0 No 33018 waits at Petworth in late September 1963 with the twice-weekly goods. There is not much traffic today and the crew have plenty of time for a cup of tea and a break before travelling the few miles to the main-line junction at Hardham. No 33018 spent its last years working from Three Bridges shed on jobs like this. Petworth station building was unusual in having diagonal planking, and was listed. It survives today as an up-market hotel with Pullman cars in the platform. *Terry Cole*

Selham station basks in the midday sun in September 1963. It has been closed since 1955 but is still largely intact. Now the goods yard is empty and the branch-line freight train will soon cease to run. The station survives to this day as a private residence. *Terry Cole*

'E4' No 32470 leaves Midhurst Tunnel with the return branch freight for Pulborough. The crew must be glad to get into the fresh air given the amount of smoke and steam billowing from the tunnel mouth. Based at Horsham shed, No 32470 was withdrawn in June 1962. *J. Grayer*

The Hayling Island branch

The Hayling Island line must be one of the most photographed in the whole of the south, and with good reason. Not only were the ex-LBSCR 'A1X' ('Terrier') locomotives that operated this picturesque line nearly 100 years old, but the summer Sunday service was so intensive that standing on the lineside a train would pass you in one direction or the other every 15 minutes. It was a railway working at the limit, with the four-coach trains packed with several hundred day-trippers and their luggage.

'A1X' No 32677 stands ready to depart from Havant in the spring of 1959, looking very smart with its copper-capped chimney. The train is formed of two BR ten-compartment 'seconds' in red livery followed by two ex-SR coaches in green. The other 'A1X' locomotive, which has brought in the train, can just be glimpsed taking water. This is a high-capacity train seating in excess of 300. (The Southdown bus in the forecourt appears to be doing good business, too.) No 32677 was one of the 'Terriers' that was broken up after being withdrawn a few months later. *Mark Warburton, courtesy of Mrs Margaret Warburton*

Another 'A1X', No 32670, crosses Langston Bridge with a similarly formed train in August 1963. A van was often attached to accommodate the number of pushchairs and prams likely to be carried. This bridge was the reason for the severe weight restriction placed on locomotives using the line. The road bridge linking the island to the mainland used to be rather ramshackle and also had a weight restriction on vehicles crossing. However, as can be seen on the right, that has now been replaced by a shiny new unrestricted bridge, and this will spell the end for the branch, which closed in November of that year. *Terry Cole*

North Hayling station served an area of caravan sites and holiday homes. 'A1X' No 32646 pulls into the station to collect some picnickers heading for a day out at Hayling Island. The first vehicle of the train is an early Bulleid coach, a side-corridor compartment composite normally to be found in a three-coach set. The locomotives on the branch almost always faced south, but here No 32646 is bunker-first towards Hayling Island. *Terry Cole collection*

'A1X' No 32661 runs along the shore between North Hayling and Hayling Island on 25 June 1961 with a motley collection of coaches and an ex-GWR 'Fruit' van at the front. It is low tide so there are vast expanses of mudflats, but at high tide the water will lap the bottom of this low embankment. This engine was originally withdrawn in 1925 but reinstated, overhauled at Eastleigh and had its air brake replaced by vacuum before being sent (with similarly fitted SR No 2655) to the Lee-on-Solent branch. As BR No 32661 it was withdrawn in April 1963. *Mark Warburton, courtesy of Mrs Margaret Warburton*

No 32677 bustles along between Langston and Havant in the late 1950s with a BR 'second' and an ex-LSWR two-coach set in tow. *Noodle Books collection*

Reading-Redhill

On a frosty New Year's Day 1965, the last day of steam-operated services on the line, 'N' Class No 31408 pulls away from Betchworth with a train for Redhill. The train consists of four Maunsell 'Restriction 1' coaches and will probably run on to Tonbridge and beyond. The Maunsell 'Moguls' provided the bulk of the motive power on this line at the time. No 31408 was among the last survivors of the class, lasting until June 1966. *Terry Cole*

On a high summer's day in 1964 you can feel the sizzling heat as 'U' Class No 31790 coasts along with a Redhill train. The shortage of coaches due to withdrawals has now got so acute that the four-coach sets normally used for this service have had to be split in half to produce two-coach sets. How they managed at peak times is anyone's guess. No 31790 was one of the original 'U' Class that were rebuilt from 'River' tanks; they could be identified by the larger driving wheel splashers, which show up in this aerial view. *Terry Cole*

British Railways Standard Class 4 No 76059 heads away from Farnborough North with a train for Redhill, the first part of which consists of an ex-SECR 'Birdcage' set. The combination of locomotive and coaches is unusual. No 76059 was not built until June 1955 and has clearly seen some service, which suggests that the picture was taken in 1956, by which time nearly all the 'Birdcage' sets had gone. *Kevin Robertson collection*

'N' Class No 31405 draws into North Camp station with a morning train for Reading on 13 September 1961. *Terry Cole collection*

Locospotters

At Victoria station immaculate 'Battle of Britain' Class No 34089 *602 Squadron* from Stewarts Lane shed awaits the 'right away' with a boat train formed of Bulleid coaches in red and cream livery. It is the mid-1950s with the engine in near original condition and carrying the first BR crest. For the excited-looking locospotters on the platform, the idea of travelling on this prestigious train would have been well nigh impossible. Being able to drive it would have been a dream as remote as going to the moon. *Terry Cole collection*

A decade later, as we near the end of steam, rebuilt 'West Country' No 34013 *Okehampton* waits at Woking station to depart with a Southampton train. In this case the engine is particularly scruffy. In contrast, the locospotter, who is carefully recording the number, is particularly well scrubbed. He is unlikely to be entertaining thoughts of becoming a steam engine driver, although in a couple of years the Americans will land on the moon! *Peter Knotley*

South Western Section shed scenes

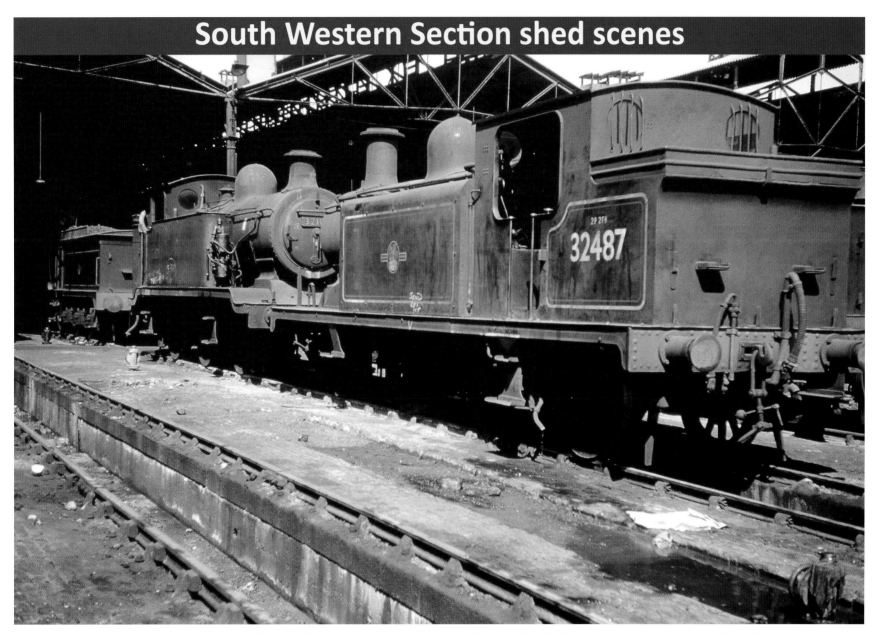

'E4' No 32487 is out of steam on the pits outside Nine Elms shed on 14 August 1961, with an unidentified 'E2' Class locomotive behind. Nine Elms usually had a couple of 'E4s' on its books, which were used for shunting. Unless wiped regularly with an oily rag, locomotives quickly developed a rusty and drab appearance, as in this case. *Terry Cole collection*

Bulleid 'West Country' 'Pacific' No 34045 *Ottery St Mary* stands resplendent outside Eastleigh running shed in 1956, having just been out-shopped from the adjacent works. The absence of any marks or dribbles on the paintwork suggests that, apart from an initial steam test at the works, she hasn't been on a trial run yet, although some faint wisps from the chimney suggest that this may be about to happen. This will likely be to either Winchester or Botley and, if all is well, she will then be returned to her home shed of Brighton in a day or two. *Terry Cole collection*

Who could fail to be impressed by the massive lines of 'G16' No 30495 as it stands outside Eastleigh shed ready for duty? The four 'G16s' were designed by Urie in 1921 for hump shunting at the recently opened Feltham marshalling yard. When these duties were taken over by diesel shunters they struggled to find alternative employment. No 30495 was one of the last two survivors, and was withdrawn at the end of 1962. *Kevin Robertson collection*

Adams '0395' Class 0-6-0 No 30566 stands outside Eastleigh running shed in the mid-1950s complete with a snowplough attached and ready to be dispatched for duty should the need arise. At major sheds it was common practice in the winter to prepare one of the venerable (and expendable) engines in this way. No 30566 eked out an existence at Eastleigh, in its last years working the Winchester goods and shunting. It ended its days as works shunter and was withdrawn in February 1959. *Terry Cole collection*

Hiding almost sheepishly alongside the shed at Basingstoke is 'N15X' Class No 32331 *Beattie*. Behind is an ex-GWR 'Mogul' that has worked through from Reading. The 1950s saw all seven members of the 'N15X' Class based at Basingstoke, where they found employment on various freight turns and on occasions took over through trains from the Western Region destined for Portsmouth. Withdrawal of these handsome engines began in early 1955, with *Beattie*, the last survivor, going in July 1957. *Terry Cole collection*

Inter-regional trains

Inter-regional trains were often operated by 'H15' Class locomotives after the withdrawal of the 'N15X' type. These mixed-traffic locomotives, of which there were four distinct types, went about their business largely unnoticed by enthusiasts. Equally at home on heavy passenger or freight trains, or for that matter on local services, they faded away in the second half of the 1950s and early '60s as dieselisation produced a surplus of locomotives. Here No 30474, withdrawn in April 1960, takes water at Basingstoke on a through train. *Terry Cole collection*

Little engines

The three tiny 'C14' locomotives started life as the engine component of LSWR railmotors. These proved to be not very successful, and the engines were subsequently rebuilt as 0-4-0 tank locomotives with Walschaerts valve gear for shunting duties around Southampton Docks and for other light work. One was transferred to Redbridge sleeper depot where it spent all its life, and is seen here carrying the Departmental number 77s. In the background work is progressing on the Eastleigh depot for the Hampshire DEMU scheme. *Kevin Robertson collection*

Eastleigh usually had two or three 'B4' locomotives in its allocation for shunting duties at Southampton Docks and also for shunting the very sharply curved goods yard at Winchester City station. There was a tiny engine shed here for overnight stabling, thus avoiding the necessity of running back and forth down the main line to Eastleigh. Designed by Adams in 1891, these powerful little engines had long and useful lives. No 30102, with its early BR crest, still carries an original Adams boiler and looks very smart as it pauses in its duties at Winchester City in 1963. *Terry Cole collection*

The Southern Railway knew a bargain when it saw one, so it snapped up some ex-US Army shunting locomotives that became available as war surplus in 1946. After minor alterations and an overhaul at Eastleigh Works, these engines were sent to work at Southampton Docks where increasing traffic was taxing the fleet of elderly shunting locos. Here is No 30069 at the docks on 19 September 1965, still carrying its first BR crest. No 30069 saw 20 years of service, not being withdrawn until the end of Southern steam in July 1967, repaying its purchase price many times over. Presumably the 'No Parking' painted on the ground did not apply to the steam engines! *Terry Cole collection*

Brighton shed maintained a couple of 'P' Class locomotives for its shed duties, moving coal wagons to the coaling crane, shunting wagons of ash, and further afield shunting the wharves at Shoreham Harbour. A low bridge and sharp bends in the track at the Harbour meant that it was only accessible by small short-wheelbase locomotives. Here No 31556 is resting in Brighton shed yard on 27 June 1960 waiting for its next duty. *Terry Cole collection*

Specials

Throughout the 1950s and '60s enthusiasts' clubs ran a great number of special trains, often featuring unusual workings.

A stranger to the South Western section, 'E1' 4-4-0 No 31067 enters Eastleigh station with the returning 'North Hampshire Downsman' on 22 May 1960. The long building forming part of Eastleigh Locomotive Works can be seen behind the engine, with the Works Offices in the building on the right behind the leading coach. *Terry Cole collection*

Another former South Eastern 4-4-0 at Eastleigh, this time 'L' Class No 31768. It is inside the Works yard with the LCGB 'South Western Limited' train on 18 September 1960. A small number of 'Ls' had been transferred to Eastleigh for a brief period in the early 1950s and after the completion of the South Eastern electrification scheme a number of these and other South Eastern engines drifted to the Western Section, but were little used. Both Nos 31768 and 31067 were withdrawn at the end of 1961. *Terry Cole collection*

'H2' 'Atlantic' No 32426 *St Alban's Head* pauses at Horsted Keynes with the 'Wealden Limited' rail tour on 14 August 1953. The load of seven Maunsell 'Restriction 1' coaches together with a Pullman car will give the engine some work to do on the 1 in 75 climb all the way to West Hoathly. However, with dry rails and a good head of steam this is well within its capabilities. After all, the 'H2s' were well used to lifting twelve or so coaches of the Newhaven boat trains up the bank out of Victoria. No 32426 was withdrawn in August 1956, but No 32424 *Beachy Head*, the last of its type, survived until April 1958. This engine is currently being reconstructed by the Bluebell Railway, so we will again see an 'Atlantic' working on this line. *Terry Cole collection*

Eastleigh area freight

'K' Class No 32345 is seen bowling along with the 10.03am Eastleigh to Fratton freight, and has just passed Botley. This is the sort of work that the 'K' Class excelled at and kept them fully occupied until all seventeen were withdrawn at the end of 1962. No 32345 was the class member put aside at the back of Three Bridges shed by the Shedmaster, hoping that it would be purchased by the Bluebell Railway. Unfortunately this never happened. *Kevin Robertson collection*

In the low afternoon sunlight 'H16' 4-6-2T No 30517 approaches Swaythling with an empty oil train bound for Fawley. As was usual, the train has 'barrier' wagons to separate the engine from its potentially explosive load. No 30517 is doing what it was designed for: working heavy transfer freights. The five engines of the class entered service in the winter of 1921 and all were withdrawn at the end of 1962. *Kevin Robertson collection*

Three-cylinder 'W' Class 2-6-4T No 31916 heads a Fawley oil train through Eastleigh. These engines were also designed for transfer freights and could often be found in the London area. At the end of their lives they were more widely scattered, with some going to Exmouth Junction for banking duties. Campbell Road bridge was a favourite gathering place for spotters as it offered a good view of the comings and goings from the shed and works as well as on the main and Portsmouth lines. No one in sight today! Perhaps it's school time. *Kevin Robertson collection*

'U' Class No 31611 catches the evening sun as it heads up the main line at Winchester Junction with a London-bound freight on 17 May 1962. *John Bailey*

Southampton

British Railways Standard Class 3 tank No 82015 is either engaged in some shunting at Southampton Central station or it may be that a van is being attached to the rear of what is a Southampton Central to Didcot service. The first two vehicles are former GWR 'Hawksworth' stock in BR red and cream livery. On the far left is a Hampshire diesel unit on a local service. *Kevin Robertson collection*

The use of BR Standard 9F locomotives on passenger trains was officially frowned upon, but No 92002 (with chalked 'King Rat' name) has been rostered to work the Poole-Newcastle through train on 20 August 1966. The reluctance to use these engines is a mystery since they were extremely powerful and had a sufficient turn of speed to be able to keep time easily with most trains. A small number were based at Eastleigh for the Fawley oil trains, but this one has worked through from the London Midland Region. The Southern men called them 'Spaceships', a soubriquet easy to understand if you have ever climbed into the cab of one from ground level! Certainly they were light years ahead of some of the Southern's antiquated fleet. In the background demolition has already started on the clock tower, the whole of Platform 1 destined to swept away and replaced with contemporary modern concrete. *Mark Warburton, courtesy of Mrs Margaret Warburton*

The eastern end of the tunnel was much less photographed. Here BR Class 5 No 73110 *The Red Knight* leaves the tunnel with a train for Waterloo and is just approaching the triangular junction at Northam where the line to Southampton Terminus diverged. *Kevin Robertson collection*

Isle of Wight

Ex-LSWR 'O2' Class No W27 *Merstone* has just left Ryde Esplanade station and is about to enter Ryde Tunnel in July 1964 with a six-coach Ventnor-line train. It was the restricted dimensions of this tunnel that limited the possibilities for replacement of these Adams-designed engines, which had been built as far back as 1889. The coaches are a mixture of ex-LBSCR and SECR stock unique to the Island. Some measure of the popularity of the Island as a holiday destination can be gauged from the fine array of coaches drawn up on the Esplanade itself, offering trips to all parts. *Terry Cole*

No W28 *Ashey* enters Ryde St John's Road station with a train for Cowes. These trains usually had a tidy four-coach formation, but here we have two ex-LBSCR brakes with an SECR saloon still in BR crimson sandwiched between them. St John's was the location for the main locomotive shed and works, and the locomotives and coaches were always immaculately maintained. *Terry Cole collection*

No W21 *Sandown* is heading away from Ryde towards Smallbrook Junction, where the Cowes and Ventnor lines diverged. In the summer the intensive service required this section to be worked as double-track, whereas in winter the signal box at Smallbrook Junction was closed and the section operated as two single lines joining at St John's Road. *Terry Cole*

Nos W26 *Whitwell* and W17 *Seaview* are heading a short goods train consisting of just two coal wagons and a brake van and are seen here approaching Brading. Double-heading on the Island was rare and usually occurred only early on a summer Saturday morning to get a locomotive to Sandown to pick up the set of coaches stabled there. Double-heading on a goods train was quite exceptional. *Terry Cole collection*

No W15 *Cowes* pauses at the north end of Ventnor station to allow its young driver to top up the oil reservoir in the Westinghouse brake pump. The Island's railways used air braking while the rest of the Southern used the vacuum brake. This picture, taken in the early 1950s, also shows the ex-LBSCR saloon coach used on 'The Tourist', which was the Island's named train. *Cowes* itself was an early withdrawal, one of three members of the 'O2' Class deemed surplus after the first round of line closures on the Island. It was withdrawn in June 1956. *Terry Cole collection*

No W24 *Calbourne* leaves Ashey station for Cowes some time in the late 1950s. Subsequently subsidence caused the station and platform to be abandoned and the latter rebuilt on a site to the right. This was originally occupied by a siding that served a nearby racecourse, both long since gone. *Terry Cole collection*

No W24 is seen again against a glorious backdrop, waiting in the station at Cowes with a train for Ryde. The locomotive has recently been given a heavy overhaul and has returned to service in unlined black. After the cessation of steam working at the end of 1966, No W24 was purchased for preservation and survives today on the Isle of Wight Steam Railway. *Terry Cole*

No W31 *Chale* has just left Medina Wharf and is steaming along the river estuary with a train of coal for Newport and Ryde sheds. Everything about the Island system was an antique, a gem. Just look at those lovely open wagons and the beautiful ex-LSWR 'Road Van' brake, long since gone from the traffic on the mainland. *Terry Cole collection*

Holmsley – an LSWR wayside station

Holmsley station was on the old line from Brockenhurst to Bournemouth that ran through Ringwood and Wimborne. When the direct line was opened via Christchurch, Holmsley found itself very much a backwater. It was served by about ten trains a day in each direction. In this photograph, taken from the road bridge, the Bournemouth West to Brockenhurst train is composed of 'M7' No 30060 propelling ex-LSWR push-pull set 33. *Terry Cole collection*

Holmsley is seen again on 31 May 1963, with 'Q' Class No 30538 arriving with a train for Bournemouth Central. The locomotive has been modified with a BR standard chimney in place of the large-diameter Bulleid one. It has not much longer to run, being withdrawn in July of that year. The station lasted a little longer, closing in 1964. *Terry Cole collection*

The Lyme Regis branch

Who could resist this lovely picture of Adams Radial tank No 30583 as it waits to run round its single-coach train in the Lyme Regis bay platform at Axminster on 3 March 1960? This class of locomotive had been introduced by the LSWR in 1882 for London suburban work, and most had been withdrawn from service in the 1920s. Of the three remaining, two were retained for working this line, which had tight 10-chain-radius curves and steep gradients, requiring a short-wheelbase but powerful locomotive. The third (this one) was sold to the East Kent Railway but was bought back by the Southern after the Second World War to assist the other two. *Mark Warburton, courtesy of Mrs Margaret Warburton*

The same engine enters Lyme Regis station with its single Maunsell 'Restriction 4' brake composite coach from Set 108 in tow. The line was rebuilt in the early 1960s to enable longer-wheelbase locomotives in the shape of the LMS-design 2-6-2 tanks to work the service. However, this was only a short reprieve for the line.
Mark Warburton, courtesy of Mrs Margaret Warburton

No 30583 with its single-coach train heads towards Lyme Regis in the low autumn light on 19 November 1960, having just crossed Cannington Viaduct. The viaduct suffered from structural problems from its construction in 1903 when the line opened. This early concrete structure was demolished when the line closed in 1965. No 30583 fared better, being purchased by the Bluebell Railway where she resides today, albeit awaiting extensive repairs. *Mark Warburton, courtesy of Mrs Margaret Warburton*

The line west to Plymouth

'S15' No 30830 enters Seaton Junction with a stopping train for Plymouth on 17 August 1963. The station had two through tracks as well as up and down platforms and a platform for the branch train to Seaton. No 30830 was one of the later Maunsell-built engines and lasted in service until July 1964. *Mark Warburton, courtesy of Mrs Margaret Warburton*

In near original condition, 'West Country' No 34015 *Exmouth* is seen here waiting at Sidmouth Junction station on 7 August 1965. The fireman has a knotted handkerchief for headgear, nice and cool and very much the fashion towards the end of steam. *Mark Warburton, courtesy of Mrs Margaret Warburton*

'N' Class No 31842 pulls away from Exeter St Davids with a Plymouth train on 9 June 1963. The locomotive was based at Exmouth Junction, which had a large allocation of the class. *Mark Warburton, courtesy of Mrs Margaret Warburton*

'O2' Class No 30182 has just arrived at Turnchapel with an RCTS special train, formed of an ex-LSWR 'Gate' set, on 2 May 1959. The surviving 'Gate' sets were allocated to Plymouth for work on the local and branch-line services. No 30182 was withdrawn in January 1960. *Mark Warburton, courtesy of Mrs Margaret Warburton*

The end of the line – Wadebridge and Padstow

The London & South Western and Great Western lines intertwined through much of Devon and Cornwall, with the LSWR finally extending as far west as Padstow on the Atlantic coast, some 260 miles from Waterloo. Here 'T9' Class No 30709 waits in the loop with a two Maunsell-design vehicles consisting a corridor brake composite and a corridor brake third, a typical formation for West Country local trains. The locomotive is of the first design with coupling rod splashes. *Alan Sainty collection*

'T9' No 30715 runs along the River Camel estuary near Wadebridge with another two-coach Maunsell set on 20 August 1957. The leading coach is interesting in that it shows the first version of the BR red and cream livery as it was applied to Southern coaches with a wide red band at the top of the side. This was quickly abandoned in favour of the neater style as shown on the second coach, with the cream section extending right to the roofline. The 'T9s' were the favoured motive power for local services in the West until replaced by the 'N' Class in the early 1960s. *Alan Sainty collection*

Wadebridge was the home of the three surviving Beattie 'Well Tanks'. Built in 1874, they were rebuilt by Adams, Urie and Maunsell, outliving their sisters by more than 60 years. The reason for their survival was the Wenford Bridge mineral line, to which they were ideally suited. The trio continued to work this line, remote from Waterloo, until replacements in the shape of three ex-GWR '1366' pannier tanks finally took over the duties in August 1962. No 30585 is standing outside Wadebridge shed on 31 May 1962, looking resplendent even though its paintwork was several years old, as shown by the fact that it still carries the early BR crest. The first '1366' has arrived, so No 30585's days are numbered. Fortunately both it and No 30587 were preserved. *Terry Cole collection*

The last steam main line

The former South Western main lines out of Waterloo were by the mid-1960s the last of such routes in the country to be operated by steam. Here rebuilt 'Merchant Navy' 'Pacific' No 35026 *Lamport and Holt Line* waits at Bournemouth Central with the 12.59 to Waterloo on 31 May 1966. The two leading vehicles are long-wheelbase LMS vans. All the 'Merchant Navy' engines were rebuilt in the second half of the 1950s, but they still looked extremely impressive. No 35026 didn't quite make it to the end of steam, being withdrawn in March of the following year. *Terry Cole collection*

Rebuilt 'West Country' No 34008 *Padstow*, devoid of its nameplates and crests, waits for 'the road' at the west end of Southampton Central with the 10.30 from Waterloo on 29 March 1967. The impressive signal gantry looks complicated but isn't. It controls the exits from three platforms, each of which has access to three routes, 'Fast', 'Slow', and 'Goods', the principal routes additionally having distant signals. *Mark Warburton, courtesy of Mrs M. Warburton*

On a glorious June day in 1967, British Railways Standard Class 5 No 73043 roars through the remains of Oakley station west of Basingstoke with a Waterloo-Salisbury train. *Terry Cole*

Pullman trains were always especially exciting. In late June 1967 one of the last down 'Bournemouth Belles', hauled by rebuilt 'West Country' 'Pacific' No 34024 *Tamar Valley* passes through Winchfield. The sidings are already being ripped out and the conductor rail is in place ready for the commencement of electric services in a few weeks' time. Unusually the train is running on the down slow line. *Terry Cole*

Flashback

Flashback to the 1950s, and here is the 'Bournemouth Belle' leaving Waterloo with original-condition 'Merchant Navy' No 35017 *Belgian Marine* in charge. The driver has gently opened the regulator and operated the sanding gear to ensure a smooth getaway. No 35017 was rebuilt in April 1957. *Terry Cole collection*

Index of locomotives